ROOTBOUND

ROOTBOUND

POEMS

MANTHIPE MOILA

UHLANGA

2025

First published in Durban, South Africa by uHlanga in 2025

UHLANGAPRESS.CO.ZA

This print-on-demand edition is distributed
outside of Southern Africa by the African Books Collective

AFRICANBOOKSCOLLECTIVE.COM

ISBN: 978-1-0370-5095-4

Edited by Nick Mulgrew
Cover illustration: "Rootbound" by Leora Joy Jones
Cover design by Jennifer Jacobs
Typesetting by Nick Mulgrew
Proofread by Karina Szczurek

The body text of this book is set in Garamond Premier Pro and Batang
The cover and inside pages also use Sofia Pro

ACKNOWLEDGEMENTS

Early versions of poems in this collection have been published in the following literary journals: "Dedication 1" (as "Dedication") in *20.35 Africa Volume 7*; "*Ceiba pentandra*" (as "Cotton Tree") in *The Hotazel Review*; "Home safe" (as "식구") in *Tupelo Quarterly*; "You think of your grandfather" (as "Severed") and "*Ficus elastica robusta*" in *New Contrast*; "You conjure a gift" (as "The Poet Conjures a Gift"), "Library", and "*Monstera Deliciosa*" in *Kalahari Review*; "21 questions with an expatriate 1" (as "21 Questions as an Expat 1–v1") in *New Coin*; "Swipe right 1" (as "Swipe Right") in *Watershed Review*; "Unsaid (황사)" (as "On the Phone or 황사") in *Stirring*; "A friend says if you were having more sex you wouldn't need the pills" (as "and her friend once said that maybe if she were having more sex she wouldn't need the pills") in *Agbowó*; "*Diospyros kaki*" (as "Persimmon"), "산 is a mountain" and "*Jacaranda mimosifolia*" in *Hole in the Head Review;* "You press your finger against a smear on the map" (as "Threads"), "Questions to ask ChatGPT when home" (as "Questions I want to ask ChatGPT when I get home") and "Mo behe fatse, o boima" in *Saranac Review;* "One therapist tells you to write a letter to your dead father" in *Thimble;* "A Korean woman teaches her grandchild to count" in *Beloit Poetry Journal;* "Another therapist says black men are wont to disappear like that" in *Pleiades Magazine;* and "Faces" in the AVBOB Poetry Project.

The illustrations that appear in "Swipe right 1" and "Swipe right 11" were designed by Ellie Bee (@ellie_beehive).

Poetry has been a space of refuge, healing, and hope for me. To be able to share my work with the world is a dream, a dream that would not have come true were it not for a village of people.

Thank you to Nick for believing in my work. The book would not be what it is without your keen eye, encouragement and insight.

Thank you to my beta readers Sihle Ntuli and Rouge Inkstone for your attention to detail, thorough feedback, and encouragement. Most of all, thank you for being my dear and kind friends. Sihle, you have been a wonderful mentor. I know you might hate me saying this, but a poorer version of this book would be living, and dying, in my laptop were it not for you. Our online workshops were instrumental to the creation of this book, and I am truly grateful.

Thank you to Charlotte Rees, Seya Fadullon, Koeun Lee, and JinKyung Ryu for weathering the storm I was throughout the process of writing this book. I would not have made it to the end without the movie nights, tea dates, and love.

Thank you to Ellie Bee for being my illustrator and friend. Thanks to Catherine for your encouragement, and for saving me when I could not figure out the formatting issues in my drafts.

Thank you to Andreas Neusch for your unwavering support, and for how well you handled my various meltdowns. Thank you for being my love and for understanding this part of me.

Much gratitude goes to Suwon Writing Group and SWAP writing group. The feedback I received helped me to sharpen many of the poems that appear within. Many thanks to the Liquid Arts Network and Kenneth May for making me feel less alone as a poet.

Thank you to my English literature professors at Rhodes University with special thanks going to Professor Sam Naidu and Dr Lynda Spencer. Thank you for believing in me and for being incredible teachers.

The first drafts of "Wilting", "Something like joy", "After the funeral", and "Damage" were composed during the *Tupelo* 30/30 online writing residency. Much thanks to Kirsten Miles for her guidance and encouragement throughout the process.

The first draft of "Fresh Water" was composed in a Poetry X Fit workshop run by Sundress Publications. Thank you for being a great resource for poets.

To my mother, Theresa Moila. You are an incredible woman. Your love, pride, and faith in me have shaped me into the poet I am today. Thank you for buying me so many books when I was little. I am a poet because you are a reader.

To little Manti. This book is for you.

CONTENTS

Dedication I

Today you happen upon a tweet by a white girl your age:
"three things black girls don't have. long hair. a boyfriend.
fathers."

You ponder the gush of girls turned ghost, the dust
that gathers them, absence marking the spot. You wonder

at this world where blackness in girl-form is a round, rotating
emptiness that only holds in a disappearing hand.

Put it in a portrait and there a hole appears. Put it on a path.
A hole appears. And in a home, it breaks like a strand breaks
(or a tooth).

Make it the size of this room, and it seems there is no one here,
sitting at this desk, writing this poem.

Playing with time

I lay the hourglass horizontal,
and watch as the sand pools
into barrows:

I hold my father's hand
as I walk down a medicine aisle.
I have asthma or something.

He tends to me; buys a salve,
ice cream, then drives home.
Except.

Where is my sister?
What is it,
exactly, that I have?

Sand pools like truth in the jaw.
I've found ways to keep my dead.
I've scented my life with him,

sandpapered mourning
into memory,
into meaning. Meaning:

Yesterday, he is not gone.
Tomorrow, he was somewhere
in that grove over there, or behind my eyes.

Today, he could love me,
and still leave.

7 ways of looking at the story of us

after Wallace Stevens

I.

On row after row of jacarandas,
aphids take in tree sap and excrete
honeydew.

2.

Purple canopies flutter
as though they are eyes.

3.

There are eyes everywhere
in that night-shattered home
where the suitcase fills
as the man lightens.

4.

Once plucked from its stem,
the flower cannot return alive.

5.

A light man weighs the same
as a single purple flower.

6.

To stuff a bag with clothing
is to fill a room with silence
long after one is gone.

7.

Once light, men find it hard
to return.

Marking home

You once made fire
out of a slick pot, stood immobile
as the flames bloomed impossibly high.

Fear clipped your every bone into place.
You had not known that such a small
thing could hold so much burning.

Once the flames were gone,
soot clung onto the wall
like a beloved done wrong.

You marked the house in shadow this way,
in the language of heat. Afterwards your family
had to leave the windows open for days.

They could hardly breathe in that place.
You could hardly breathe.

Conjugating loss

I am trying to lose my loss like I lost him.

He lost his way to me.

We lost our beating
breaths.

I let loose my loss in the house.
It makes a noise like an angry child.
I try to place it on the table –
          it kicks   it screams.
My family cannot look me in the eyes.
I have lost my sense of the room.

I might lose all who tire of this leitmotif.
I too have lost interest in the opera of it all.

I want to pull loss out of the mouth
where it sits like a milk tooth that won't
give. The pain is louder than it should be.
I wish I could hush it to sleep.

I hope loss loosens one day
though by then – I am certain –
I will have lost too much.

Jacaranda mimosifolia

You have given up your abandonment
the way a boy jumping into a river gives up his shoes.
You have given up your hurt, your want;
that ancient skin, that old wound.
There are moments like this when you walk
the streets of Johannesburg with friends or family,
bare of yourself, crushing the fallen
flowers beneath your school shoes.

You do not know you are practicing forgiveness,
nor do you know it will all be for naught.
The trees bloomed in Pretoria days ago,
and you are smelling time already gone:
a belated world of violet, one that your father
will slip into and never return from.

Faces

On some days, the sky is a mirror I cannot reach.
Touching it would be grazing your frail face.
The river looks like an ocean
though there are no oceans here
just as there are no fathers.

On other days, everything has a face:
the clocks, the shoes, bodies of water.
I picture yours and my mind dissembles.
It gives you frailty; it gifts you a second chance;
it surrenders my blank stare at your guarded gate.

We are only a stone's deft throw away
from a small fracture; two stones
from a splintering world
where you are a man with many faces,
many lives, and I am in all of them.

Home language

A friend asks you how to say 'she' in Sesotho
and in your haste to grab for the word you slip
into a world thick with honey
and your words are like teeth dissolving
in the sugar that constrains your tongue.

How to say it is always too late to reach the words?
You want and want and want to retch language
(if that's what it takes).

O lahlehile: *she is lost.*
Ha a tsebe: *she doesn't know.*
Ke mosadi: *she is a woman.*

You don't say 'she' in Sesotho. You rebuke –

O tletse tsoekere: *she is covered in sugar.*
Ha a tsebe: *the air cloys with her desperation.*
She is o lahlehile *a woman who claws for words,*
o lahlehile.

Home safe

So many saids are unthinged when one grows up anti-
conversation and pro-elephants in the room.

Only in certain contexts is it okay to bring up
the animals: a tiger roams the streets of Joburg –   HAHA!

Today the silence in the kitchen
took to the air like a rock dove –   :/

In this den, tenants walk through one another,
shooing questions that bubble up like

What do you think, sis? Is water wet?
Would you wear the ocean, corpses and all?

What of your own oceans of thought?
What lays its eggs there and dies of exhaustion?

Are you tired? Are you scared?
Do we hate each other now?   :/ :/ :/ :/ :/ :/ :/ :/

On days when the hue of a screen is colder than usual
and the floor begins to turn to water beneath the feet,

I think of my family home in Meadowlands
and want to do as I had never dared before: lie belly up

on the red stoep, press against its rigid surface,
knowing that it will refuse to let up.

Sting

after Safia Elhillo

earthenware chunks | on the kitchen tiles
on bare feet smears of blood | the offences mount
beget tears beget a stinging | in the air violence sings but

you know it intimately | an open palm is not a fist
an open palm harbours love | cuts only where it needs and
girls heal like trees heal | wood callouses over the wound

but what if you

were thorned instead | grew many-spined
under the canopy | clustered near an edge
that hooks back | where no hands venture

there girls cut | there girls smash bone
into glabrous skin | hand over china
while they taunt | and sting

Ceiba pentandra

the cotton is exhalation against my skin
    I rip through breath and smile   pocket the small hardened hearts

I have no concept of them as living   think only that they are pretty
    and will always be there

I come home one day to find stumps   in the place of warm snow
    and soon after   the earth pouts as if to say

see where you hurt me   I want to echo its pain
    see where you hurt   but don't

I cannot point   to a particular place on my body
    my wound a travelling spasm

but the trees   they know exactly where   and want recompense
  for every missing layer of dead bark

living phloem   sapwood   heartwood
  pith   all of it

had I known   I wouldn't have sat by the mailbox
  waiting for a letter   that would never come

I would instead have filled it with little brown hearts   until they spilled out
  onto the street   grew hilly with pain

a mound that could swallow a house   two houses
  three houses: a mountain of want   looming like a stubborn wish

Fresh water

I came
> as a voyager
>> of sky. I came
>> having descended
>>> from this miracle
>>>> of flight
> with a yearning
> verging
>> on sorrow.

I ask
> for a small thing:
>> sojourn, a place
>> to lay my spent feet.
>>> What fare do I lay
>>>> before you?
>> A spot of blood?
> Stories of voyage?

The journey
> has been long,
>> my friend.
>>> Do me
>> this one
> one justice.

The poet conjures a gift

For the young girl who sits neatly on the bed
and receives news of the estranged father's passing,

you conjure a leave-taking. See how there is a newly acquired stiffness.
He moves more slowly than usual, embraces like a fleeting thing.

Be warned: when you finally see him, he will be impassive,
adorned in a rigidity that cannot be undone. And when,

as a woman, you move to a scorching city in South Korea,
he will return to you again and again: a man with no features,

a creature far too still, and always turning his head away,
just so.

21 questions with an expatriate I

after Sumita Chakraborty

1. Would you call this running?

I thought I could fashion a woman
out of the scraps of me:
that if I pricked the lips, I would cum;
that if I pricked the belly, I wouldn't tire;
if I pricked the eyes, I would cry the moment
I heard of my father's death.

2. What would you call this then?

I wanted to needle myself thicker,
widen the outlines
so I'd be harder to hide from.

3. What have you collected here?

Stories of the dead. More longing.
Truth is… before I got hooked
on Murder Mystery & Make-up Mondays,
I thought I could kill a man.
I feel I've lost a weapon.
Bailey blankets on the make-up,
speaks of men and women who have butchered,
leaving me bare-handed and wide-eyed.

4.*When will you stop draping the world in catastrophe?*

When I'm no longer a coward.

5. *Have you fallen in love yet?*

It's not that kind of story.

6. *Cowards don't fall in love.*

That's not a question.

4.*Okay, let's try it like this. Is there really a monster in the road? It's not a
plastic bag, or garbage, an abandoned toy?*

In the months before he died
my father kept a city-wide berth
between himself and his daughters.

7. *Is this the life you pictured?*

I will not be tricked into complacency
by my lover's voice.
I will not flit towards any fiend
all cavalier like a girl loved right.

8. When will you stop writing about your father?

I know I'm always grumbling about him
but even I can admit
that manhood buried daddy
like if you piled all the pebbles
from Geoje Island on top of one body
then told it to stand.

Dactylonomy

PALM

He slides his finger along the slick ceiling of your body, the mat beneath you belches. You both laugh. Later his body will warn: *I intend to move through you the way I have moved through cities I came to love and left anyway,* but as he enters, you find him in places you didn't expect. Your stomach. Your chest. Your palm.

THUMB

And you think *fuck I have a lover* and want to finger your way into his smile, yet you only know how to work with teeth. He doesn't like the biting nor your suggestion that he flick you across the forehead when you get too excited. So you tell him that there's this doctor you see bi-monthly, that you cannot sleep and trudge through the fog of your days. Everything always so far away.

INDEX

Then come the days when you wonder if he cares about you at all and he if he is wasting his time with you.

MIDDLE

But look at these slim hands of yours. You didn't come here to fuss
or fight – he had such cool eyes. You would rather he pluck the
pleasure out of you, fingers wet. Sing you the song he wrote for another
woman, fingers nimble.

RING

You don't want his honesty, like that one time on the red line when he
casually pictured his life without you, and the pain struck you in the
thighs, left a ringing in your ears. Before you came here you had never
even ridden the Gautrain, had pictured your life in Daegu differently
because of a Sally Wen Mao poem, pictured yourself riding a bus from
heartbreak to oblivion, *Lovewave* blasting in the background.

PINKIE

Most nights he lays you on your belly as if to say: *I cannot give you
much, not even the promise that I will not wound you. But here are your
stomach, your chest, your palm. Here is the world of your body. Here you
are, a little less far away.*

Creative endeavours for the sane

Paint pens that smash laughter
out of the body without shattering.

Do you remember? The polka-dot art.
I'm trying for pottery. Woodwork.

Knitting loneliness out of the day.
Sewing seams onto my cracking

voice. Seems like you have left me
writing your face onto a skywashed

landscape. Mending cracks with
golden tributaries. Wondering

how I got to this river without
your photography. Scrapbooking.

I'm drowning in paper, baby.
I'm drawing in light and breath

and I cannot say for sure but it seems
you have left me watching birds alight,

left me dancing to your name alone.

First winter

Cold moves
through the room,
an apparition.
You pace, calling
it a dance.

*

Like a child,
you want to show
Cold the something
you swallowed
when your hurting
got the best of you.

*

Cold is only interested
in turning your palms
the colour of pus,
or bending you
into yourself.

*

You are well-bent
like a river
that stopped moving.

*

You beg Cold to take
you out or leave.
It merely bares its teeth.

*

A friend says if you were having more sex you wouldn't need the pills

outside the light show presses itself against my windows as I lie beside my bed wreathed by
washes of colour my trembling hands pressed against my lips I am a far-cry from the women

frolicking in palace courtyards   adorned in hanbok vests large
sparkling skirts plastic   garlands or redolent in
streetlight sheen the   children who squeal as
night sinks Daegu   I am to everyone a
daughter of myth a   faraway thing in the
morning I try to   blink the world into
a kind of order hold   it briefly lose it
sleeplessness has me seeing   double again I try to tell
myself *this way I can have two of*   *everything* and the blueberries might

multiply and my hips widen and my lover's hands be everywhere desire too might double into
entendre so that when I think *touch* instead of *the live wire myself* follows instead of *myself*
into extinction him no tablets only clinging to another knowing soon the world will be beautiful

Swipe right I

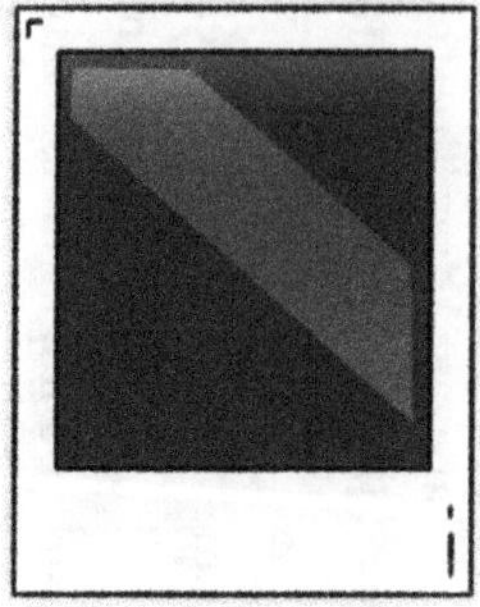

**, 26

 kms away

BIO

small-voiced
tender-breasted
tightly-wound

remembers the Korean word for face
by picturing a room
full of ghoulish leers

speaks about home in abstractions
wants love to be concrete
and textured right

brittle like bone
left to soak in soda   (says soda now)
neat-limbed but

mind the fissures
mind the pebbled teeth
mind the soft gummy tissue

might open
if you promise
to crack first

Unsaid (황사)

Instead of
    the dust is a harsh yellow
    that stains everything after each rain.
    Lately there is something caught in my throat
    and it threatens a din that would shatter
    even the wailing of a mourning creature.

Instead of
    it gathered speck by speck,
    sometimes when I speak it comes out
    in a noxious puff that sinks to the ground
    and captures the footprints of those
    walking away from me.

Instead of
    when I was young, I was so afraid of the sun
    lest it strip me of my yellow. But now
    there are days when I am a pit where yellow
    collects and layers the length of my throat,
    the pockets of my lungs.

Instead of
    did you know that the sun is not yellow?
    It is all the colours.
    All of them.

I smile a white smile:
I'm fine, thanks. How are you?

A Korean woman teaches her grandchild to count

She points to the motorcycles
parked along the subway
and shouts 일곱! at the seventh.
The boy approximates 이고!
and you imagine the refraction of colour
which breaks open in them joy –
the woman, the boy,
windborne bubbles against the sky –
as it opens in you your own dearth.
The scene is now a garble of gesticulation,
and the triumph of "열" enters you
not as sound but as a soft heat.

The closest you get to ten in Sesotho
is *tharo*; to heat, *mollo,* as in fire,
as in there is only a lick left,
only memory, only time:
the time in your sister's nduma when the wick
wouldn't flame until the seventh try,
and finally, your sister lit the mphepho
and called on your deceased grandmother,
her voice gravelly, her speech spotless,
and yours like a dappled leaf
clutching onto the last flashes of red,
dying, nearly dead.

You had forgotten to press your words tight
between two pages, thinking nothing of it,

not even *here is a path you might uncover*
to find your way back. Instead,
you turned to find the past
had recoiled so far
you could only approximate
a course to all the words that had fallen out
and extend a trembling hand until your sister said,
It's okay, you can do it in English.
Freckled in shame, laying your hand on your lap,
you opened your mouth to speak:

The smell of home

The land is soft like a nail plate
hounded by acrylic polymers and drills.
Bark could come apart in my fingers a fine dust.
The rain was harsh last night,
a troposphere of reprimand.

Small swamps now make up the city floor,
and the smell of earth tendrils
its way around the trunk of my body.
I want to open my mouth to it,
to breathe harder, insisting on this pale blue
smell in this dense and dampened world.

But despite all this water, why
that constant smell of burning?

Wilting

You want to be one less thing to carry.
You think of your love as sweetened clove tea:
sapid, a dark liquid that seeps you into a heavy sleep.

You want your honey to take you to bed as you wilt,
his lilt in your ear, his hand caressing your coarse belly hair,
for the weight of fatigue to curl away like smoke.

You want to wake unburdened next to your love,
your skin reading his as light that enters the room of you,
your own body so light you forget that it's there.

Severed

Somewhere in the world it is decades ago
and a group of men cut through Nyasaland, Rhodesia,

puncture their way into the Union of South Africa
blanketed by night. It is terrifying, the night:

though it conceals, it gashes its way into the hearts of exiles
and stays. But where to turn when sunshine betrays each figure?

I never knew to ask if the sharp colours hurt you, Mkhulu.

I now wonder if you feared the sun's rays the same way
the elderly feared the young man chosen to lighten the tribal load

by carving them out of the bigger picture.
Did you ever happen upon the elders' weight pressing down

a dark cloud of vermillion? Was it a reminder,
Mkhulu, of all the things you had to sever?

Threads

To you the stranger

is still warm on the wall, their

smudged inky print, full of breath, marking

the subway map. You think of them, full-fledged

and made of bone, as they trace their way across the

expanse of the city – a teacher, a writer, a student? – flustered,

wondering, *am I going the right direction?* And having found their

place, having inked their way onto the underbelly of Seoul, did they

feel more fixed to this capital than all the other fingers that have ever

touched the inside of the car / the glass panes / the map, most of them

wiped clean by now? Or did they know the truth of the vast city

as it spread out before them, mycelia of metal and concrete,

routes affixed, thread after thread? Did they know that they

– made of bone and all – are in truth merely the fruit

of the animal that it spits out for a time:

temporary and small.

Helianthus

The length of your laughter is a sunflower field.
Does this mean you are so beautiful
I cannot take you in all at once?
No matter. I wish to take but softly, politely.

Bring your breath, bring your laughter,
bring your wide hands and dense flora.
Drip sleep into me, my love. Soften my bones.
The body is too heavy with itself.

It is time to go to bed.

Monstera deliciosa

this evening you think
of your aunt's magnificent garden
and want her to teach you how
to get more perforations on your monstera
     though you desire to speak only about nodes
       the unfurling of the leaves   aerial roots
       and she might ask if you ever think of starting a family
         and you about propagating in water
           and she about how often you think about Jesus
           and you about how to keep leaves from browning
             and she about when you are coming home
              and you about the leaves
               their sheen
               how did
               she get
               them to
               grow so
               big

21 questions with an expatriate II

after Sumita Chakraborty

9. On a scale of one to lonely – "no" being the wrong answer –
how lonely are you?

I don't understand the question.

10. What's your favourite meal here?

I hunger for a version of myself
who is more patient, smarter,
a cup size bigger.

11. Where have you been?

Busan, Jeonju, Geoje, Seoul,
Gyeongju, out of my mind, Ulsan.

12. Would you date a Korean guy?

Sure.

13. You just want to call someone oppa, don't you?

Bite me.

14. Be careful of the meat.

That isn't a question.

14. Is this how you pictured your life?

That isn't a question either.

15. How do you deal with pain?

By making strange noises.

15. I'm sorry. Can I get a do-over?

Yes.

15. How do you deal with pleasure?

By making strange noises.

16. The world is coming to an end. How have you dealt with that?

I salted plastic to taste,
took red meat off my grocery list
for a bit. Got a manicure.

16. I don't understand.

My manicurist shoulders my broken questions
with the kindness of a teacher who enjoys their job.
She offered me a mask during the panic,
often tells me I am beautiful.
Means it. Warns me not to die.
Whenever she is undoing last month's work,
and the specks of plastic fly towards her nose,
I think: what is it, exactly,
that constitutes a person?

16. Is this the best you can do?

On Sunday, Durban's air was worse than Daegu's.
I had been naïve enough
to think that I would
return home to clear skies.
How much of the world is left for us to eat?

17. Are you disappointed in yourself for having retreated into vanity?

Where else would I go
now that I have some money?

Alternate titles for black tax

after Danez Smith

1. blood that smells strange now
2. rootbound
3. the house is always falling
4. pay up
5. bound for elsewhere
6. ∞ a lemniscate
7. it's complicated
8. a slow painful crawl
9. it really is complicated
10. a pit in the stomach
11. a hunger
12. quicksand but slower
13. all the words for loop
14. the reason you are here
15. the things that you missed when you were a girl
16. perhaps in the end you will forgive one another
17. to hold
18. grace

One therapist tells you to write a letter to your dead father

I.

In Korean the word for apple
and apology sound the same.

2.

Twice I've stood in an orchard.
Once as a girl in Lesotho
where there was no DStv
but come nighttime there were so many skies
it almost made up for the silence.

The second time I was just outside of Daegu.
I had paid to pick apples,
could have as many as would fit into my basket.
I spent most of the day eyeing those
out of reach.

3.

Sometimes I picture you as an apple orchard.
All those potential forgivenesses
begging to be wrested from the branch:
사과 and 사과 and 사과

Sure, the hanja is different,
but in a poem what is the difference
between an apple orchard and you
closing the distance between us?

Library

You sit in a library in Yongsan
and a wide-eyed girl gapes at you.
She is perplexed by the fabric around
your head, the dark skin, the too-big eyes.

She tries to map your face,
strains to find the place it leads to.
The girl's mom tugs at her gently.
You smile but then remember

the mask. Can the little girl tell?
Does she see the strange, hidden
expression and think, *smile*?
Or will she stand rooted

against her mother's soft pleas,
insisting, *Masked stranger,*
why are your features all wrong?
Why do you struggle so to speak?

타다 / tada

after Emily Jungmin Yoon

On the train my plastic mane goes rogue, unbuttoning.
Almost everyone bends towards their phone.
Shyness blunts all efforts at touch.

On the platform the cold shocks all my exposed bits.
I want to reach under my skin and flush out each icicle,
in my feet melt away every temptation to fly.

I can almost hear it. Not black ice. Ice that declares 'tada'
    when it is too late.
타다: to burn, to ride, to be sensitive to the cold/heat.
탔어: I rode the burn. Like heat it marks my skin but
    doesn't quite disappear.

Ficus elastica robusta

In your Joburg yard
you are startled by a now-quiet being,
bare-leaved after the hailstorm.

In some places ice falls quietly,
gnawing at the skin.
In others it strikes at flesh.

You want to sheathe
the pitted wounds,
smooth on a sticky salve.

When you touched it,
it was like a coarse dark hand,
fingers hidden in soil.

In your Seoul apartment, you have one.
You didn't realise when you bought it
what you were calling home to.

Questions to ask ChatGPT

1.

At Deoksugung, the leaves flutter toward the exit as if to usher me
out. Earlier my path was carpeted by them. Yet now they tumble
forward, hushing softly.

Note: Can something be both dead and alive?

2.

There are days I feel I'm a leaf, its midrib off-center, like I was born
pointing the wrong way, my veins mangled and stark.

Note: *If I were a leaf, would you carry me? How far? For how long?*

3.

Some homes have serrated edges, are always drying of hunger. *Pay
up, pay up.* This is their song. It is never a bird, it's *pay up* picking
up where it left off.

*Clear notes. Note: How do I stop wishing home were cordate,
a hushed thing I could flutter toward without fear of being crushed?*

In search of soil

To be curved by the cold
into a posture of begging.

To twist the petiole
so the wide hand faces down.

To be surrounded by dead things
at a distance from kin and kind.

When you were born,
it was not to the earth.

Instead, it was to this prison
of bending. You want...

but the woman who looks after you
is sad today, all the windows

are closed. The air is fathomless.
You cannot move.

There is so much room.
None of it for you.

Train to 대화

I chase after you
as you get on the train to Daehwa.
There is a crowd of people between us.
I tear your name from my mouth
but all that comes out is birdsong.
Thinking I am a bird,
the crowd begins to hiss.
I peck away at them.

When I get to the train door,
it opens to a field of snow
where your shoeprints are vanishing.
I curse the snow for turning you
into a spectre, and in response
it falls more feverishly.
It makes so much
silence, you would think
the world was ending.

Alternative titles for pay up

INVOICE

ISSUED TO: ▮▮▮▮▮▮▮▮▮▮   INVOICE NO: ▮▮▮▮▮▮▮▮▮▮

PAY TO: ▮▮▮▮▮▮▮▮▮▮

DESCRIPTION	QTY	TOTAL

They come demanding your hair.
They demand whole strands:
the cortex, the cuticle, the bulb
as proof of life. They want the brow
and lash, the vellus hair that
glints yellow in certain light.

	ALL	ALL

You think you might miss the two hairs
protruding from your throat
that a lover mistook for debris
and tried to pull out. You might miss
the unruly underarms that once sent
a grown man screaming.

	ALL	ALL

Others, too: the pubic hairs spread
over your labia getting caught
in your underwear, the pain of it.
Those same hairs in your lover's teeth,
the humour with which he lifts them
from his tongue and dives back into you.

                              ALL   ALL

What would you smooth down
with prayer hands and loose from the shaft?
What would you curl and layer and bat?
What would you twirl when you are anxious
or bored, hand gravitating
to throat or kitchen or crown?

                              ALL   ALL

You should say no.
But when your hand drops to your throat,
you find nothing, and remember
that you said yes
a long time ago.

                              ALL   ALL

____

                              TOTAL: ALL

Swipe right II

**, 28

 kms away

BIO

Don't picture this
One moment the air is air   the next the air is thick smoke   and everyone directs
their hungry eyes at me   the honey they will feast on to escape to a new home

Picture me as I demand
Picture me as the falling ginkgoes that line the sidewalk   not their bilobed leaves
the pungent fruit that never draws a hand   a tongue

Except for yours   I want yours tracing the borders of my ink   pocket me, darling
let me make a mess against your flap your fabric   just this once let me be the one heavy
with nectar seeking refuge   finding you

Another therapist says black men are wont
to disappear like that

It is written, prophesied into ruins with whetted blades.
Were you not weaned off father like the others?

Why were you fed milk until such a big age? Your father was
a person. A man beholden to something beyond you. His blackness,

for one example. The colour of disappearance, for another.
Why this desire to break these monuments of absence into mourning?

Have you ever seen a strangler fig? Accustomed yourself to its
grip? Let the branches attach? Vine? Hollow out that sour feeling?

Black girl, go ahead. Let it make you pretty with its gaping.
Let blackness swallow black men as it does. Let what will be, be.

21 questions with an expatriate III

after Sumita Chakraborty

18. How's your Korean?

> Whenever I am asked how many languages I speak,
> I don't mention all the words that I've misplaced.
> At least I still know how to say sun in five different ways:
> sun, letsatsi, ilanga, son, 해.

19. How are the people?

> I don't know much about people.

20. Have you learned how to be a person yet?

> I get up to marvel
> at the long-armed octopus
> pressing itself against the glass.
>
> Later, the server grabs one out of the tank,
> cooks it alive,
> and I wonder if I should be eating
> something I can't bear to watch die.
>
> With nakji-bokkeum on our tongues,
> my date and I speak about friendship,

vegetarianism,
that one scene in *Oldboy*.

Later, tired of my mask,
I strip down to my skeleton.
My date doesn't care for the theatrics
but thinks I have pretty bones.

...is that what it means to be a person?

21. When will you return?

I want to make a ramshackle home
out of all the words I know.
It will be sun-dappled,
holy. Whole.

Small poem

you know
your pain is not
the size of
a city

your pain isn't big
the size of a continent
a country
a road

but why wasn't love bigger

you want clean pain
neater smaller

and buried by skin pain
the smallest thing

Mo behe fatše o boima

there is a poem somewhere in here
there is a father in that poem who
the smaller he gets the heavier he gets
so that by the time he disappears
he is the heaviest

and that poem ends with a thud

Damage

What we call damage is a kind
of triumph: a fissure turned

crack turned fragmented slab.
Agape, we watch the furore of roots

as they force the concrete to move aside.
We think of how we can undo

the damage, how to tame the roots back.
We view it as a form of aggression,

a desire to conquer, to swallow up a house
or neighbourhood, or perhaps us.

What if it is language? What if the tree is speaking
through the roots in search of another

of its kind, seeking someone in this desolate
landscape to share its secrets with?

'M'e oa ka

1.

You spill into the room
like a pool of sunlight in late autumn,
your hearty laugh, your ready smile,
your face a place of treasures.

2.

When you ululate
your voice rings clear through,
as though you were calling
to some other world.
Perhaps sometimes you are –
to your mother, to hers.

3.

It carries, your voice, like you carried
me when you cast your first ballot.
You the woman who breaks the grey sky
and lines the clouds in brilliant white.

4.

You were named after a father
who clears the way –
Pachuma Pasi Pali Mtika Chamayembe –
your eyes hazelnut crowned by green,
an opening to the world.

After the funeral and that unfamiliar stiffness we could not
recognise as kin, we return to our lives with a soft kind of relief.
The world spills onto a chair, then slips off. We do with the
emptiness what we always have done: fill it with the green ink
of the Han, hoping that its undulations carry us through,
knowing that there is something there, something like a man
in a balaclava on a bike cupping his lips to shout obscenities,
unfurling his arms like wings. There's an angel, there is flying,
there is the possibility we will know each other again.

Something like joy

A knot you just untangled
reroutes itself into chaos.
The chocolate you licked
off just-washed hands
tastes of soap. Ink lines all
your territories into the
wrong shape and you
are left to wonder what
we do all of this for.

What if, instead,
you thought of strands
you have saved, the delight
of having cocoa and sugar
on your fingers? What if
you thought of yourself
as being without territories,
borderless, steeped
in something like joy?

Walking home thinking of love

On the way home from swimming class the streetlights along
    the walking path are like dragon blood trees
                                erect little bodies opened to the sky
        and he   another lesson in how to open the body
Despite my terror   I want his damp and slick   so I do it
                                throw wild and dive into him
    finally boundless   spreading further and further apart from myself
                buoyant   floating upward
        until I am a celestial body   seeing now   the lights along
                                the walking path are
        celestial bodies too   lighting my way to a trail
                where something awaits

            The two of us   hand in hand
    now one hand   now a walking path
                        now a dragon blood tree   now
            vaster than every sky
                    every galaxy

Adulting (a fairy tale)

Your head falls on the desk in slumber.
Cold tea spills, a lake of brown that drips
onto the wooden floor and snakes
towards another crack.

The desktop winces. Tabs pop open
like startled eyes. It doesn't matter.
You have turned into a log
on the forest floor.

Moss begins to dust your skin green.
You are a tunnel now
and all see your open body,
your little forests.

You are a house of houses, a dream
woman. In your disappearing,
you will birth lichen and
liverwort and fruiting bodies.

And the light will touch you where
something more
than a tired life can, and will, bloom.

Jeju

I am afraid too much sight can kill me.
— Feng Sun Chen

The wooden door opens to a white rooftop terrace
overlooking the water.
Still autumn refuses to alight.
The light is almost too much to bear.
How do they bear it, those tetrapods, the sea?
What is it like to absorb wave after wave and stay standing?
I remember the time I was so sad I could hardly stand my life.

But the tangerines, I say. But my sticky fingers wet with juice.
But the wind that lifts my heavy afro.
I am tickled.   I am dizzy.
There is so much light it almost hurts.

Diospyros kaki

While waiting for friends in an alleyway
you might come upon a persimmon tree,
its branches bare save for unripe fruit.

You might let your eyes trace
what seems like lines of decay
that taper off into bursts of orange.

You might think there is a sweetness
at the heart of all that bruising,
there is a creature that made it through.

Cheonggyecheon, Jonggak

The signs proclaim:
Let's walk, Seoul! We are a walking city!
But I am frozen in this posture of want,
my desire simple –
for time to stop so I can steal
into that concrete ravine,
blithe,
my fingers stained maroon
by sweet berry tea,
my tongue stinging.

And I would turn my back
on the cafés, and tall glass buildings,
even the Avenue of Youth;
would dip my toes into the stream to tickle
the moss HELLO,
and leave a trail of water as I slip under
Samilgyo,
stopping by the north wall
of Welcome to Paradise
to pluck hydrangea from painted stone
and stick it in my mane,

then whisper my secrets
to the grove,
blue and orange and green
with mirth,

and it would whisper to me
the secret of how
to conjure more stream.

So, I would
conjure more stream
and it would stream
ahead of me. Water.
Actual water
that goes on
and on and only stops
when I tell it to.

산 is a mountain

after Emily Dickinson

And when you search desperately for *Bliss*
it comes to you as an alleyway that *is*
paved green-grey, sloping upward *but*
tapering off at a slant; this *bliss*
feints towards a dead-end *and*
really leads to true green, to *breath*:
a false sun which is a mountain which is *but*
a friend who holds space for you, for yet more *breath*.

Monstera deliciosa variegata

In the photograph a woman dances
with a slight bend at the knees.
She is satined both in silver and light,
is light as a head free of hair,
light as starlight in the city.

If I were to suspend time
to this quivering melody,
could I avoid the sinking world
and all its gravity?
Would I find behind the wall
of the kitchen or in the back garden
more music?

Ma, I wish to make you
a variegated world,
with enough green to sustain us all,
enough white to stun,
and a pattern that makes everyone marvel
at the mystery of how
things turned out this good.

Dedication II

Today you sit with K on a rooftop in Haebangchon
and the buildings around you are like mountains, Namsan Tower

pointing skyward as though to command them higher.
Your fingers curl, and you think *thaba*: mountain/be happy;

think *haebang:* liberation, *chon*: village.
Eventually, K finds you seats inside where you write

while looking out the window, mountain after mountain
protruding into view – thaba, thaba...

Later, you will melt the wax beads and seal this poem inside,
entrust it to the ocean of time, hoping that one

of our future selves grabs it from the depths, and opens
it to find – *thaba, you are here* – some kind of freedom.

NOTES

Though the subject matter differs greatly, this collection as a whole draws inspiration from *Everything is a deathly flower* by Maneo Mohale.

p. 14, "7 ways of looking at the story of us"
   This poem draws its title and inspiration from Wallace Steven's "Thirteen Ways of Looking at a Blackbird".

p. 17, "Conjugating Loss"
   This poem draws inspiration from "Teaching My Mother English over the Phone" by Eloisa Amezcua: "she asks me how to conjugate [...] love".

p. 23, "Sting"
   A contrapuntal poem inspired by "Yasmeen" by Safia Elhillo.

pp. 29, 49 & 65, "21 questions with an expatriate" series
   This poem's form was inspired by "Basic Questions" by Sumita Chakraborty.

p. 38, "Swipe right 1"
   얼굴: 'face' in Korean, pronounced similarly to *all-ghoul.*

p. 40, "Unsaid (황사)"
   황사: 'yellow dust' in Korean, pronounced *hwang sa*; a natural phenomenon caused by dust blowing from the deserts of Northern China and Mongolia into South Korea, creating dangerous levels of air pollution. (Source: Brendan Pickering, "Hwang Sa (Yellow Dust)," *Asia Society,* https://asiasociety.org/korea/hwang-sa-yellow-dust)

p.41, "A Korean woman teaches her grandchild to count"
   일곱: 'seven' in Korean, pronounced *eel-gop*.
   이고: not a word, pronounced *ee-go*.
   열: 'ten' in Korean, also heat, pronounced *yol*.
   tharo: 'three' in Sesotho.
   nduma: a structure wherein a medicine woman/man conducts their
      spiritual practice and gives consultations.
   mphepho: African sage.

p. 52, "Alternate titles for black tax"
   This poem draws inspiration from "alternate names for black boys"
      by Danez Smith.

p. 53, "One therapist tells you to write a letter to your dead father"
   사과: 'apple' or 'apology' in Korean, pronounced *sa-gwa*.

p. 59, "Train to 대화"
   대화: Daehwa, a neighbourhood just outside of Seoul.
      The same word translates to 'conversation'.

p. 69, "Small poem"
   A contrapuntal poem inspired by "Why Are You So Extra?"
      by Alexa Patrick.

p. 70, "Mo behe fatše o boima"
   'Put him down, he is heavy' in Sesotho.

p. 72, "'M'e oa ka"
   'My mother' in Sesotho.

p. 77, "Jeju"

The epigraph is from "The Living" by Feng Sun Cheng.
Reprinted with permission from the collection *Butcher's Tree*
(Black Ocean, 2012).

p. 81, "산 is a mountain"

A golden shovel poem that uses a line from "Rouge Gagne" by Emily
Dickinson: *Bliss is but bliss, and breath but breath!*
산: 'mountain' in Korean, pronounced similarly to *sun*.